Spot, The Red Fox That Lived Under GramB and Poppa's Porch

Tommy Keith

Copyright © 2016 Tommy Keith

All images are copyrighted and were taken by Tommy or Becky Keith as the foxes lived and played in our yard. We live in the South Run subdivision in **Fairfax Station, Va.**, which is located next to **Burke Lake Park** in Fairfax County.

Images used in this book, and many others we took of this red fox family, can be purchased at:
www.500px.com/tommykeith

Also on Instagram:
https://www.instagram.com/tomkeith/

ISBN-13:
978-1536814552

ISBN-10:
1536814555

© 2016 tommy keith

Hi, my name is Spot. I am a red fox, the most common fox in America.

I know you are probably wondering why my name is Spot, since that is usually a name for a dog. I got my name from GramB when she noticed the spots on my face and tail and legs. In case you are wondering who GramB is, she and Poppa are the owners of the porch I am sitting on!

I was born under this very porch along with my brothers and sisters — Little Red, Copper, Long Socks, and Little Gray — early this spring.

© 2016 Tommy Keith

Isn't my Mama beautiful? I think that is why GramB named my Mama the Red Beauty. Most red foxes have red-orange or yellow-orange coats. I think all red foxes are beautiful no matter what their color! Female foxes are called vixens and male foxes are called dogs. Baby red foxes like us are called kits or pups or cubs.

When Mama knew she was going to have babies, she needed to find a quiet place where we would not be easily seen and we would be safe. GramB's front porch is lined with shrubs all the way across, so my Mama could come and go easily. Mama burrowed under the porch and made her den there, where she gave birth to us.

GramB and Poppa wondered if Mama had made a home under the porch, because one day they came home and saw Mama sitting right next to their house. Another fox had her baby kits here four years earlier. When Poppa looked closely around the porch he found the three entrances to our den!

Mama was pregnant for about two months before she gave birth to us under the porch. At first we were blind and could not hear, so we stayed close to Mama and were protected by her warm body and her coat of red-orange fur.

Mama nursed us for those first few weeks. While we drank Mama's milk, our Daddy would bring food to Mama to eat so she could stay and protect us.

The first time GramB and Poppa saw all of us was when GramB looked out the front room window and saw Mama nursing us on the front porch. Boy, was GramB surprised!

GramB immediately grabbed the camera and took a picture and then went and told Poppa to come look. Here's the picture she took.

Mama was feeding all five of us! We were about a month old. I bet you have never looked out your front window to see a red fox nursing her kits before!

After I finished drinking my milk, I ran back over the edge of the porch near the den opening and then looked back up to see what everyone else was doing. Poppa took my picture again. He sure took a lot of pictures!

My coat was mostly brown and my eyes were blue when I was born. I stayed close to our den at first. Mama made sure of that.

If we started wandering too far from the den, Mama had a special bark to let us know we might be in danger and to get back to the safety of our den. She was a very good and protective mama!

That's Little Gray. Do you like his gray coat and blue eyes? We all looked like this until we were about a month old. Mama had all five of us kits early in the spring. Some vixens have four to six kits if there will be plenty of food to live on. I was lucky — I had four brothers and sisters to play with! When food is scarce, some vixens only give birth to one or two kits. Since GramB and Poppa live in the woods, there was plenty to eat.

It wasn't too long before we started playing farther and farther from the den opening. But the den opening was just a couple of feet away, so we felt safe.

When Mama saw me out of the den, she came over and sat down and I ran and pounced right on top of her tail.

I tried to get Mama to play with me because I was the only one out of the den. Mama didn't seem to want to play, so I bit her leg to see what she would do.

It wasn't long before two of my sister kits ran out of the den and pounced right on top of me! We had a lot of fun pouncing on each other and play fighting. That is how we learned to hunt and defend ourselves.

Play fighting with my siblings wore me out and made me sleepy!

Mama got tired too. It's a lot of work to raise and feed five kits!

Mama stayed close as we played, and she would stand right
next to us when she thought danger might be approaching.

When we were about a month old, our blue eyes started turning
to amber and our gray coats started turning more red-orange.

It wasn't long before all of my brothers and sisters — Long Socks, Little Gray, Little Red, and Copper — were brave enough to come out and play right in the middle of the yard.

Sometimes Mama stayed close by to protect us and other times she was off hunting food for us to eat. We were growing very fast and we were always hungry; it took a lot of hunting to keep us fed.

Mama is a very good hunter. She knows exactly how to sneak up and pounce on smaller animals. Mama is sneaking up on a squirrel to catch for our dinner.

As soon as Mama brought the squirrel to us to eat, my sister Copper ran off with the squirrel so she could have it all to herself!

Some people think we only eat meat, but we will eat just about anything. We will eat worms or bugs or fruits or vegetables, and sometimes pizza crusts when they are left on the front porch!

We have excellent hearing, so we can hear bugs and even worms moving. Little Gray and Little Red were listening to hear the insects moving in the grass.

One day, the lady across the street put slices of bread out for the birds to eat, but Mama sneaked up and grabbed the bread before the birds ever saw it. As soon as I saw Mama coming with a mouthful, I ran up to get my share!

One day, Poppa left a piece of pizza crust on the porch to see if we would eat it. Of course we would! Like I said, we will eat almost anything! Long Socks found the pizza first and enjoyed every bite.

Even though we were eating everything we could find, we still liked our Mama's milk the best! Every time Mama would come back from hunting, we would run to her to nurse and get our milk.

We let Mama know how much we loved her by giving her lots of hugs! It felt really good when she would hug us back.

Some days, it was hard to get enough milk with all five of us fighting to get under Mama. So sometimes I would go back and try to get another drink of milk when my sibling kits went off to play.

I always gave Mama a kiss to thank her for her patience and for letting me get another sip of milk.

We got pretty good at sneaking up and pouncing on each other, because we were always play-fighting. When Little Gray had grown up and his coat had changed color a little bit, he sneaked up on Little Red and Long Socks and pounced right on top of both of them.

It almost looks like Long Socks is flying. We are getting really good at pouncing these days!

It seemed like all we did was eat, sleep, and play-fight!

My Mama has very good hearing, so she knew GramB and Poppa were always watching through the window and that they were always taking pictures. They tried to be quiet and hide, but Mama heard them and kept an eye on them too.

For the longest time, we all played close together near one of the den openings.

But as we got braver and more comfortable, we started playing all over the yard. Sometimes we ran clear into the neighbor's yard and then chased each other back to our Mama. Did you know we could run very fast? Red foxes can run 30 miles per hour!

We ran all the way back to Mama and hung out under our favorite tree in the corner of the yard. I got back to Mama first!

Once we got a little older, Mama decided to take us out to hunt with her. We mostly hunted at night, but sometimes we hunted in the daytime too. Mama made sure she took us out one at a time so she could teach each of us how to hunt. Red foxes hunt alone and not in packs like coyotes. Today it was my turn to follow her so she could teach me some new hunting tricks.

By the time we got back from hunting, it was pouring rain and everyone was hungry. So Mama went right up on GramB and Poppa's porch and let us all enjoy some milk.

We were just getting settled into drinking our milk when the neighbor's dogs came outside and started barking. So Mama scooted off and told us all to go to the den.

But by this time, we were getting more grown and Mama was trying to wean us so we would not be drinking her milk much longer. She wanted us to be able to catch our own food and not rely on her. We were growing up so fast.

Mama had taken us out one by one to hunt, and she taught us well. Though we had loved playing in GramB and Poppa's front yard, it was time for us to all move away and find our own homes.

I bet GramB and Poppa still look out their front-room window everyday hoping to take more pictures of us. But we have moved on, though maybe we will come back and visit again someday.

And maybe, just maybe, I'll come back and have my kits under this same porch. We always felt safe playing in that yard. GramB and Poppa always watched from inside the house and never tried to run us off. I think they enjoyed having us around as much as we felt comfortable being there.

I have a feeling Poppa will still have his camera handy so he can take pictures of my family someday!

© 2016 tommy keith

ABOUT TOMMY KEITH

I love the outdoors. I am a husband, father, grandpa (they call me Poppa), Harley rider, business owner, author and photographer. My wife and I took all of these pictures as the foxes lived and played in our yard. We live in the South Run subdivision in Fairfax Station, Va., which is located next to Burke Lake Park in Fairfax County.

Images used in this book, and many others we took of this red fox family, can be purchased at:
www.500px.com/tommykeith
Also on Instagram:
https://www.instagram.com/tomkeith/

DEDICATION AND THANKS

This book is dedicated to our Grandkits, Geoffrey, Abby, James, Andrew and those still to come.

Thank you to my amazing wife, Becky, who tolerates, and at the same time, encourages my constant picture taking. Becky also helped me select the pictures and edit this book.

Thank you to our wonderful editor, Sally-Anne Cleveland!

Made in the USA
Lexington, KY
18 September 2016